HO

WITH DIFFICULT PEOPLE

Control the Situation! Overcome Your Annoying
and Frustrating Coworkers

(Strategies to Deal With People You Can't Stand)

Hugh Griffin

Published by Sharon Lohan

How to Deal With Difficult People: Control the Situation!

Overcome Your Annoying and Frustrating Coworkers

(Strategies to Deal With People You Can't Stand)

ISBN 978-1-990334-71-9

Legal & Disclaimer

The information contained in this book is not designed to replace or take the place of any form of medicine or professional medical advice. The information in this book has been provided for educational and entertainment purposes only.

The information contained in this book has been compiled from sources deemed reliable, and it is accurate to the best of the Author's knowledge; however, the Author cannot guarantee its accuracy and validity and cannot be held liable for any errors or omissions. Changes are periodically made to this book. You must consult your doctor or get professional medical advice before using any of the

Table of Contents

Introduction

This book contains proven steps and strategies on how to deal with difficult people.

Difficult people are difficult in every sense of the word; it is difficult to get along with them, communicate, work, or even live with them. Difficult people normally range from being mildly irritating to being almost impossible to deal with, and the annoying part is that we all have someone in our life that we can describe as difficult. They can be your family members, friends, workmates, or even spouses. This means you cannot avoid interacting with them. Thus, the only possible solution is to learn how to deal with the difficult people in your life.

This book will equip you with the practical tools and skills you need to interact with, and manage difficult friends, family, relatives, neighbors, and colleagues in your day-to-day life.

Thanks again for downloading this book, I hope you enjoy it!

Chapter 1: Don't Be Afraid Of Delegation

Delegation… for some managers, it's a dirty word. It's an unwelcome reminder that they should relinquish some of their control and pass along tasks, responsibility – and authority - to others. That's a scary thing to do. It's also something that many modern managers in the UK are particularly bad at.

For novice managers, delegation is a skill and an art that you are most likely unfamiliar with and will have to work hard to adopt. Chances are it will also be one of the things that you will find the hardest to do.

It should be easy, right? After all, logically you need to delegate to your team in order to make sure the work gets done. In some environments, such as the fast-paced pressure of a kitchen or restaurant, it would seem easy to do; everyone has their assigned place and their tasks. Yet I bet you that no matter how good at delegation you think you are, there is still more that you could be doing.

The fact is that you are PAID to delegate; it's your job as the boss to manage other people and their time, as well as your own, in the most effective way. That means encouraging others to step up to do the jobs you shouldn't be doing. After all, think of it from the company's point of view – you're the boss now; you are paid more than those below you to do a different role.

A manager is paid to think of the overall operation of their store, restaurant or factory. To do that, they need to have a bird's eye view of the business; that's just not possible if you're sweating the little stuff. Delegate the detail and keep an eye on everyone's roles, but don't try to do their job for them.

Think of yourself as a conductor in an orchestra. You're responsible for the entire performance; it's your job to make sure everyone plays well and works together to make an amazing piece of music. You can do that by leading from the front, just as a conductor does.

You cannot do that, however, by spending half the performance playing the clarinet yourself because you worry that someone else can't play it as well as you. Focusing on just one little area leaves the entire team rudderless, which is when other mistakes happen. What will you do when the Oboe misses his cue because you weren't there to give it, or the drums come in too early? Or the pianist plays a bum note? Will you now try to play the Oboe, drums and piano?

That's called fire fighting, my friend. Fire fighting is when you're so busy rushing from one little task to the next that you don't have any time to oversee the big picture, in this case the entire orchestra's performance. Go back to being a conductor; your team will be much more productive and your results will improve.

It's what you are paid for, after all. You are simply too expensive to do the tasks that others can do. It's a waste of their resources, money, not to mention your own time. That's why delegation is important.

If you're working ever longer hours and still have the frustrating feeling that there just isn't enough time in the day, you need to learn the art of delegation. In fact, let me stress something here that could save your sanity in months or years to come; moving up to a managerial position doesn't automatically mean that you should be working more hours.

It's true. The most efficient manager doesn't work longer hours; they work smarter. They take advantage of delegation to get the job done in the most efficient way possible; they also let themselves have a life outside of work as well. So if you have to stay later and later at work, come in earlier or even put in hours on the weekend when you normally wouldn't do just to keep up, don't assume it's normal or even acceptable. Your boss may be happy to let you think it is, but I have news for you – it's most certainly not. As such, delegation is not just good management; it could also be a career life saver.

Delegation is also valued by your team and can be a great motivator. A recent survey of 3,200 administrative professionals cited "delegating meaningful tasks" as one of the top ten most desired qualities in a manager or boss. So why don't we know how to do it? Probably because a significant proportion of senior managers in the UK have little management training before they take on their new and challenging roles.

I'm not going to lie to you. For a new manager, delegation is frightening. New or inexperienced managers in particular have a tendency to think the worst is going to happen if they let go of the reins.

Delegation means essentially giving your trust and authority to others and allowing them to run with it. It's no use delegating a task but then insisting that the employee comes to you for every decision that needs to be made; effective delegation delegates the decisions – and the authority to make those decisions – too. While it's great for encouraging employees to use their initiative, the results – or lack of – will still come down on your head. It's no wonder so many managers have a phobia-like fear of the lack of control associated with delegation.

At the same time, if they're honest, a great many bosses who struggle with delegation may well have other personal reasons to blame – insecure managers will be reluctant to train anyone else up to do their job in case it makes them more easily replaceable; others still may feel threatened by specific employees who seem to be more qualified than they are, while nervous supervisors may simply not like telling people what to do.

Extensive research has shown that the biggest obstacle to delegation is the boss. They may think they are protecting their turf, but really they are potentially signing their managerial death warrant. Jobs, careers and even businesses have been lost because of poor or non-existent delegation.

If you struggle to do it for yourself, however, think of your team. It's no exaggeration to say that delegation can transform the ethos, energy and effectiveness of a whole department; it can also help or hinder someone's career prospects. Choosing to delegate is a statement to your staff; it underpins your commitment to allow and encourage your team to develop and grow to their full potential. Think of it this way: you're not just a manger, you're also a coach.

Delegation should never be a battle between boss and employees; if you have a team who reject your delegation attempts, you have bigger problems at hand. We'll come onto how to deal with those in the second part of this book.

I understand delegation doesn't come naturally so with that in mind, listen out for your reaction when it comes to delegation.

For instance, do you use any of these excuses?

"I just don't have the time to explain it."

"My employees don't have the right experience for this task/ no-one is capable of doing the work."

"If you want a job done right, do it yourself."

"My team already has too much to do."

"My employees don't want the extra responsibility."

Do any of these sound familiar? Be honest: if you find yourself uttering any of these immortal lines, ask yourself – are these things really true? Most of the time, they're not. They're just excuses to cover up your own insecurities. Like I said, the biggest barrier to effective delegation is you.

If you secretly worry about an employee messing up the work for which you will be accountable or fear that delegation is a sign that you can't manage everything, that's perfectly normal – but counterproductive. Likewise, if you hesitate to give employees extra work and responsibility in case they won't like you, I'll refer you back to the stand I took at the beginning of this book: you're not in management to make friends.

So assuming you are committed to making the most of your new role and embracing delegation, where do you start? Let's get to the detail:

What Should you Delegate?

First, the easy answer: you should delegate any of those tasks or jobs that you used to do before you were promoted. Give them to someone more junior, just as you were junior when you did them. Don't fool yourself that because you were very good at your old job, someone else cannot do it just as well. In fact, it's now your job to make sure they do. There's a natural instinct to want to be the best at something; if you were the best in your department, shop or business at your old job and were promoted internally, you may not want someone else to take that away from you, even though you have moved on. That reticence may be understandable, but it's not helpful and it's certainly not fair to your team. Any job that you have experience in should be the easiest for you to explain to others.

If someone has more experience that you in a certain task or field, use it. Delegate these tasks to them. It doesn't mean you abdicate responsibility for them – as the boss, you're not allowed to do that – but it does mean that you acknowledge their talents and skills.

Delegate decisions: I touched on it earlier but delegation won't work unless you give people the freedom and authority to make their own decisions. If they have to run back to you every time something happens, you're not giving them the power they need to truly develop and fulfil the task at hand. You will, of course, need to determine the limits or restrictions on these decisions so that you feel confident that nothing disastrous will happen without your knowledge.

Try to share the delegation around – both the good and the 'dirty jobs'. There may well be times when you have to ask people to do something outside of their usual job descriptions, such as asking a member of staff to clean the toilets, perhaps because the usual cleaner is unwell. If this is the case, make sure you share these tasks around and don't always make a case of giving it to the person you don't like/ is most junior/ who you think deserves bringing down a peg or two. Ask them as a favour and point out that you would really appreciate their help; demonstrate that you are also willing to 'get your hands dirty' in other ways. Try to foster a team spirit so that they know they need to pull together in a crisis. If the employee point blank refuses to help out or to do anything that isn't in their job description, point out that in today's environment everyone has to do additional tasks. Oh and make sure your job descriptions actually do state that you may require people to do additional tasks as and when needed at your discretion!

Don't take advantage too much though; it really isn't fair if you hire them to do one job and then ask them to do another. Don't be bloody minded for the sake of it; while it may be acceptable to ask a member of staff to stand in for the cleaner for one or two days, if you make no effort to find a new cleaner and it continues for weeks, you are taking advantage. If you believe you are making acceptable requests, however, and the employee continues to be obstructive, make a note of it and raise it at their performance review. Highlight it as a concern that needs to be addressed; make it a target. If you need to take disciplinary action on this one, make sure that you have all your ducks in a row - and that your job descriptions cover you for this eventuality. Otherwise you are lining yourself up for an unfair dismissal case that the employee might very well win.

As time management guru David Allen says in Getting Things Done, The Art of Stress Free Productivity, keep in mind the two minute rule. In short, if you can do something yourself in two minutes or less, do it and delegate the rest. As a general rule of thumb, if it's going to take you longer than two minutes to explain a two-minute task to someone else, choose the quickest option and do it yourself. The exception here is if you want to hand over a recurring task or something that should be part of their job in the long run; by delegating the task now, it will save you time over the long haul so it's worth doing.

A quick word on what **NOT** to delegate: You should never delegate anything confidential or sensitive to employees or the company. You should also avoid delegating those extra responsibilities that specifically came with your new managerial role – team-building, performance reviews and motivation, for instance.

So, How Should you Delegate?

The most important part of delegation is communication. Poorly communicated tasks will ensure delegation is a failure. Make sure the employee knows what you want them to do, they have the authority to make the decisions necessary to achieve it and they know how to do it.

If in doubt, think SMART:

☐ Specific

☐ Measurable

☐Agreed

☐Realistic

☐Time-bound

Give them as much information as they need to do the job and the guidelines they must follow. Be wary, however, of defining their task too rigidly; the purpose of delegation is not just to get the job done, but to encourage initiative in your team members. Stephen R. Covey in his book 7 Habits of Highly Effective People describes the best form of delegation as 'stewardship delegation'. Stewardship delegation defines the desired outcome and the rules the employee must work by, but leaves the details to the employee who will do the work. This compares to 'gopher delegation' where every step is dictated to such a degree that you might as well do it yourself. Don't demotivate the employee before they even start.

Let's take a look at some of the phrases you could use when you're delegating. These are designed to encourage individuals to want to take on the tasks you are giving them and to feel as if they have been rewarded by the act of delegation in the first place:

Good Phrases to Use

"I chose you because you have the perfect skills for this task."

- You are letting them know why you chose them specifically for the job at hand and giving them recognition for their skills. You are also showing confidence in their abilities.

"I want to give you more responsibility because I think you've earned it."

- You are showing them that you trust their judgement and feel they are ready to step up. By phrasing it this way, you demonstrate that extra responsibility is a positive thing which needs to be earned.

"This will give you more experience of..."

"This will make you more visible to upper management."

- Demonstrate a benefit to the employee; make sure it's a genuine one. Point out what they can learn from the task and how it could open doors for them or develop their career in the future.

"You've helped mentor a lot of new staff and you've got a strong idea of what skills new candidates need. I'd like you to screen these potential job candidates and select who you think are the best five for the job."

- Here you are informing the employee of the outcome that you want, as opposed to outlining the methodology or procedure they should use. You are allowing them the freedom to do it their way. You are also showing them that their past exemplary work has given them the opportunity to develop further in their career.

"What do you think we should do?"

How do you think we should do it/ proceed?"

- Employees are much more motivated when they feel a part of something and believe that their views are listened to. Telling them of the task that you want to delegate and getting their input into how it should be done will encourage them to take the job on and be proud of it.

Phrases to Avoid

 "Anyone could do it."

"This is easy."

- This is an instant de-motivator; if anyone could do it, or if it is easy, this is not a special assignment or one that is related to their skills.

"I don't want to do this anymore."

- You are not asking them to do a task that is urgently needed; you simply can't be bothered to do something anymore.

"I think you should be able to do it."

"I know you're not good at x, y or z but you…"

- It's crucial that you show confidence in your employee when delegating a task.

Some other tips:

Make sure you choose the best employee to delegate each particular task to; consider their experience, work load and aptitude. Don't be afraid of giving them more work, however; just make sure they priorities their to-do list and report back to you regularly.

Delegate gradually. Too daunting a first task will only engender demotivation. Start slowly; give the employee one task that then leads onto another and another. Not only will they become more confident, you'll also become more convinced of their ability at the same time.

Keep an eye on the employee but don't pester them or ask them for updates on the hoof. This is the surest way to make them feel harassed. Arrange regular set meetings where the employee knows they must bring you up to speed with the developments so far. In those meetings, it is important that you don't make decisions for the employee which they could make themselves. If they ask for help, encourage them to work through the problem themselves and steer them towards the right path but don't do the work for them.

Enable failure. This is often the hardest concept for a novice manager to grasp; sometimes, failure is ok. See failure as a learning tool and give the employee the chance to learn from his or her mistakes. Encourage them to think of solutions to the problem at hand and learn from it. Likewise, don't judge the employee according to how you would do the job; let them find their own way. People will fail but it's important that they learn from that failure. If you're nervous about allowing this, take it slow; manage it carefully for the first few weeks and then move on.

Remember always that delegation is crucial in staff motivation. If your team is tense and demoralised, the chances are that your delegation needs some work, as Robert, a team leader at a large superstore can attest to.

"I thought I was doing really well in my new role; I felt on top of things, we were getting good solid results and sales and the staff seemed happy, if not exactly bouncing off the walls with energy. I was proud of how I was handling the many varied demands in my new role; if I couldn't get everything done on my list, it was because there just wasn't enough time in the day to cope with the workload.

"It's true that I was working incredibly long hours and never really had any free time, but I thought that was just a consequence of stepping up. I was never told to do those hours; I made the decision to do them so I could keep on top of what I needed to do. After all, surely everyone takes on more hours with more responsibility. Once things settled down I could get my life back.

"I went into a performance review with my immediate boss after my first three months confident that he could find nothing wrong with my performance; how wrong I was. It turned out that I wasn't just expected to do everything on the list that wasn't yet getting done, but I was meant to do other things as well; how would I find the time to do that?

"When I asked him in frustration how I could do it all, he just looked at me calmly and said: 'You're not supposed to do it all. That's what you have a team for.' For the next ten minutes, he spoke to me about delegation and all of a sudden it made sense.

"When I was promoted, I somehow retained my old tasks – probably because I felt comfortable with them – as well as my new ones. That was my first mistake. I made many more. I was so scared of failing in my new job that I was reluctant to allow anyone to do anything that wasn't first approved by me. Without knowing it, I held people back while making life even more difficult for myself at the same time.

"After that chat with my boss, I drew a plan of action at home that night. I decided what I wanted to delegate and to whom. I won't deny that I was still fearful of things not working out, but I was determined to try. Almost from that very next day I saw a change in morale; suddenly it was easier to get people enthused.

"I still have times even now when I want to take back a task, or selfishly keep it for myself so it can be done the way I want it done, but do you know what? As long as it is done and done well, it doesn't matter how they came to achieve it. I've learnt that much. I've also learnt that delegation is the key to a happy and thriving team.

"When I think back to how controlling I was before, I realise that I wasn't just storing up future problems for myself, I was depriving them of the chance to become something more. I wasn't just failing myself, I was failing the team."

This chapter should hopefully have convinced you of the importance of delegation with regard to your own career prospects and your team's. There's just one thought that I want to leave you with that I cannot stress enough. It's the key to whether your delegation will live or die – and to whether your reign as a manager will be successful or not. Yes, it really is that important. It's also incredibly simple...

Don't abdicate responsibility.

I touched on this in passing earlier but it's worth stressing again. As the boss, you don't have the luxury of abdicating responsibility for a job just because you have delegated it. You'll need to walk the fine line between allowing the employee authority to make decisions and yet still monitoring the job to ensure it is completed effectively. Likewise, you need to find a way to offer support when needed without undermining the employee or taking over. Don't ignore the importance of this, or bury your head in the sand: no matter who does what, you

28

are still accountable for everything your team does.

If you haven't communicated effectively or monitored the project sufficiently, any catastrophic mistakes or failures are yours alone to bear. It's another reason management is lonely at the top, but if you wholeheartedly embrace delegation – in the way that it is intended to be used – you'll also benefit from your team's successes as well.

After all, there is one thing to remember about delegation that tends to cut through all the worries and fears about giving away your authority: if you train people up to be able to replace you one day, you will be free for promotion – again!

Chapter 2: Lighten Conversations With A Dash Of Appropriate Humor

Humor is a powerful tool in communication. In fact, if it weren't, then why are so many comedians making a lot of money? Remember, when combined with wit and timing, humor is something that can make anyone's day much better.

Let me tell you a story about a classmate of mine and I a few years back when I was still in college. It was the first day of class and I was a bit earlier than usual. I looked around for someone to talk to and I thought it was a good idea to greet this grumpy-looking man sitting alone in the corner of the room. Obviously, it wasn't such a good idea because he just ignored me. However, instead of feeling offended, I said, "Not having a good day, huh?" While this may not be that funny, it did break the ice and the two of us started talking to each other. A few years later, we're still friends and hang out every once in a while.

When used the right way, humor can be the bridge that some difficult people need to go from hard to deal with to being friendly.

Besides, when you're funny, it's easy for you to show that you're always composed and calm. Those are two qualities that will make your life so much easier when dealing with difficult people.

Be a Leader

There's a saying that not everybody is born a leader. Do you know what I think of that? That's just plain stupid. I mean, nobody is really born anything. Sure, some people are born smarter or are more genetically blessed, but that's pretty much it.

Keep in mind, nobody is born what they really want to be. Our qualities, attitudes, skills and even talents are all things that we eventually cultivate as we grow up. While you may think that leading only applies to organizations, this is not exactly the case.

Leading happens all the time, especially when you're talking to people. This is because when we communicate, two or more people always tend to take turns leading and following.

Unfortunately, difficult people love to lead. To add to that, they like leading by setting a negative tone and like to talk about what's wrong over and over again. As mentioned in previous tips, that's not exactly going to help when it comes to solving problems.

If this ever happens to you, don't let it drag on. Interrupt the difficult person trying to make things negative as soon as possible. Do something drastic like changing the topic or redirecting the conversation. Do everything that you have to do to go from follower to leader and from then on, try to keep the conversation positive and lively.

If the conversation is positive, the whole thing becomes more constructive and it will be easier to solve the problems.

Who knows, the difficult person may understand how he or she is affecting everything negatively and may start being more positive the next time around.

Confrontation

If there's anything that you've learned from previous tips, it's that bullies will be bullies, and that the majority of the difficult people that we're talking about are and will always be bullies. They'll keep on bullying you too if you don't do something about it.

Fortunately, all bullies have one thing in common and it's that they're afraid of confrontation. They'll only prey on those they see as weak. If you remain passive and compliant, you're making yourself a likely target.

What do you do? You do the opposite! You show some backbone. You stand up for yourself and show the bully that you're not going to cave in just like that. If you do this, the bully will often back down. And no, I'm not just talking about bullies in the schoolyard, but rather bullies in general. This includes relatives, co-workers, employers and bullies in other places and situations.

Tom Hiddleston once said, "When people don't like themselves very much, they have to make up for it. The classic bully was actually a victim first." This holds true for most cases. What's worse is that they may have had it worse than you. Their life experience is no excuse to bully you, but it may help you understand bullies a little bit more.

However, even though I'm encouraging the confrontation of bullies, by no means should you do this without thinking of your safety first. It's important to remember that bullies, despite most being cowards, are still bullies.

During confrontations, it's best to have someone with you. If that's not possible, try to arm yourself in case something goes wrong. After all, some bullies may resort to physical means to try to prove their so-called superiority. If ever that happens, be sure to keep a paper trail to keep track of any inappropriate behaviour. Who knows, the bully may not only try to physically abuse you, but also blackmail you.

Remember, you're adults now. You can always use legal measures if the bully does something inappropriate, or if escalation is the only way to prevent the bully from bullying you or any other person in the workplace or around them.

Besides, even if you're the one bullied, that doesn't mean that you have to stand up to the bully alone. Much like how you're encouraged to tell teachers when you get bullied, the same applies when you're adults. However, teachers are replaced with law enforcers or lawyers this time around.

Chapter 3: Categories Of Difficult People And It's Classifications

Perfectionists

When I first started my company, it used to take me at least 12 hours to produce an article that I thought was worthy of being published. My writers would send in their work, and I spent sleepless nights trying to edit and come up with the "perfect" piece. The thing with a perfectionist personality is that nothing will ever be good enough. You will find ways to look for mistakes, even where there aren't any.

One thing that is important to note is that being a perfectionist is something that is crippling. There may be that person in the office that is so passionate about their work is bursting with ideas but unfortunately cannot express them with unbridled freedom. It is the same thing with perfectionism – it holds you back because of anxiety, a sense of haunting unfulfillment, and depression.

Well, so many people think that being a perfectionist is about harboring the desire to be perfect alone. The truth is that it goes beyond that. You are merely choosing to derive your self-worth from the world around you. That explains why you end up being overly sensitive to criticism or rejection, and you end up believing that you are a stupid worthless failure or bad.

If you are a people-pleaser, then that is a sign of being a perfectionist. The thing is, seeking perfection often causes people anxiety because all they are thinking of is how they can be the best. You desire to control the outcome of your actions just so that you can gain approval, acceptance, praise, and rewards.

But do you think that the perfectionist in your office knows that they are obsessive and cynical in their behaviors? Certainly not! Just like I was, they may not even know that they are perfectionists, let alone putting in efforts to stop.

So, how do you deal with them?

Well, the thing with a perfectionist is that they are often detail-oriented, negative towards others, and sticklers for the rules. If your boss, subordinate, or colleague is this kind of person, the ways to handle them vary widely.

Dealing with a perfectionist subordinate

The thing that these people have in common is that they all notice details and have very high standards that an average person cannot even breath close. To deal with them, you must;

Avoid giving them large project scopes

One thing that is important to note is that most perfectionists have admirable qualities that many people find worthy. However, there are quite a few of them who choose to hone skills on a small component of a project instead of paying attention to the bigger picture. If you work with these kinds of people, it is helpful to assign them to select tasks based on their skillet.

In other words, you can opt to give them projects that are limited in scope but are detail-oriented. The truth is that most of them are not willing to delegate tasks, and the best thing you can do is allow them to work on projects independently – as long as the project requires a unified vision to complete.

Appeal to their sense of vanity and empathy

What if your employee is a neurotic or narcissistic perfectionist? Well, these kinds of people have a powerful desire to please others. The most effective way to motivate them is to explain to them how their style of work affects those in the team. Ensure that you phrase it in such a way that they realize you already know they have high standards – and that you appreciate these high standards they hold.

You may say things like, "Mary, you have very high standards, just like me. That is what this company is all about. However, remember that good morale is essential for good productivity." What you are merely telling them is that the best way forward is to give a compliment even where they feel like there is something to criticize.

Appeal to their self-interest

What you will note is that several perfectionists want to be so perfect – either because of internal or external motivation. If you find that a subordinate is treating their colleagues poorly in the workplace just because they are perfectionists, remind them that such kind of people struggles hard to climb up the ladder. Remind them that the more they raise the ranks, the more they have to learn how to compromise for the sake of the whole team. Say something like, "I know you have been trying to ensure details of the project have been attended to, and the book does everything. That is great because if one is going to get the big things right, they will have to start by getting the little ones right. You are on the right track to the big things. However, what you need to remember as you progress is that the upper rank is about looking at the bigger picture. This means that if you focus too hard on getting 100% success, that will only bog you down. Have a vision for the next phase and not just a tunnel vision that might cost you more than you can pay for."

When you put it like that, they will start to realize that 100% is not all that counts, but achieving the primary goal, however, the approach you take is what counts at the end of the day.

When you are dealing with a perfectionist colleague, it is paramount that you know when to take a stand and when to let go. While this is something difficult to attain, you must take time to think about how important the issue at hand is so that you know when the time is right to take a stand.

The first thing is for you to keep a perspective. Agreeing with what your boss says does not mean that you have to follow their suggestions to the letter. While this seems at first as being passive, simply say yes and move on with your life. This will reduce the chances of stirring up conflict and stress. Saying yes to what they say does not mean that you have given away your power. It is quite the opposite because this will set you free from paying attention to their demands.

Ask them what it is they would like to do differently

Did you know that criticism is one of the best ways' perfectionists use to hide their insecurities? While this is upsetting, it always helps to remember that this is their defensive mechanism. They may just be lashing out because they feel insecure about one thing or the other.

When you take time to ask them what their preferred methods of going about something is, you are merely disarming those insecurities. Try telling them that you care about their emotions. When they realize that you understand their feelings, they will start to feel secure – and less critical in the future. Say things like, "I see that you are upset about the outcome of this project. Would you like a chance to talk about it?"

Stick to your guns

Think about it, is the issue you and your colleague have relevant? If so, then you are right to stick to your guns. There is a chance that no one at the office is aware that your colleague is a perfectionist. If there is something you consider relevant to you and disagree on, then realize that it is your right to spit it out.

Don't get me wrong- by disagreeing, I don't mean that you should argue about it. Simply state what it is that you disagree with and then move on. You don't have to let that disagreement to define the kind of relationship you both have. Simply say things like, "I understand where you are coming from. I just think that our perspectives are quite different on this one."

If they stir up an argument, simply walk away. No one will blame you for walking away from a case.

Keep distance

One of the simplest ways you can stay away from conflict is keeping a safe distance from it. If you have to work together on a project, simply remind them that each one of you has their roles and responsibilities and that you will do yours to your supervisor's satisfaction and not theirs.

You always have the choice of disengaging. If they keep going on and on about inconsequential details, all you have to do is remain noncommittal. Simply make your escape with such statements as "Huh, I didn't know you felt that way."

Dealing with a perfectionist supervisor

This is simply what I often refer to as 'managing up.' The main aim of doing this is to help you identify the personality of your boss – their strengths and weaknesses – so that you can effectively tailor your conversation to match theirs.

The problem with a perfectionist boss is that they always desire to be in charge. At first, this may be self-evident, but the truth is that it is not. Ask them what their expectations are. When you do this, you are giving them an enhanced feeling of being in control. This also protects you from providing an arbitrary response. While perfectionism may be unreasonable – inherently – you must try as much as possible not to be. The trick is for you to pay attention to their start points, endpoints, or boundaries to lower the chances of getting them angry.

Push information their way

Once you know what it is that your perfectionist boss is looking for, simply give them – don't wait until they ask for it. The more you offer them a wealth of information they are interested in, even before they can ask for it, the less likely they will think of you as a flawed person. This way, you escape conflict by being in the right place, at the right time doing the right thing. Remember, out of sight, out of mind!

Be at peace with the fact that there is only so much you can do

The fact that you are a subordinate means that you have very little influence on your superior's personality traits. There are times when they are critical and others overly-critical. But the good news is that you can still earn their trust and respect. The only downside to that is that you might have to endure too many interactions that are draining. Just do what is right and let the rest be decided by fate!

Seek mentorship and support elsewhere

Now, you have a perfectionist boss who is supposed to be your mentor, but the truth is that they have set unreasonable standards you cannot attain. This means that if you take them as mentors, you will strain yourself too much just to earn their praise.

Perfectionists make very poor mentors!

While we all need support at one point or another, you cannot find it from your perfectionist boss. The truth is that such people tend to hurt your self-image even more. The last thing you want is having your self-worth determined by people who already think that everyone but them is worthy.

Jump ship when you have to

Consider that dealing with such a boss is something that you have to adapt to and not accept it indefinitely. You must know when to cut the cord. The trick is for you to earn their recommendation and move on. This might mean that you seek employment elsewhere.

Start planning your exit strategy as early as you can.

Control Freaks

Let us consider the following situations;

You want to hang out with a friend you met recently, but then your long-term friend insists that you should not because you have not known them well enough to hang out with. This friend asks that if you are going to hang out, you must tell them where exactly you will be meeting when - date and time.

Does this sound familiar?

Well, the truth is that this has happened to us – whether by partners, friends, or family members.

Such kind of people is referred to as control freaks. Dealing with such types of people is not fun – no matter how much they mean to you. It could be that they are doing it because their heart is in the right place, or they mean you no harm, but this is entirely lethal force you don't want to mess with.

You may be thinking, but who exactly is a control freak? Well, a control freak simply refers to perfectionists who feel vulnerable to anything that seems to them as uncontrollable.

The term "control freak" is a psychology-related slang. It describes a person who wants to dictate what everyone does and how everything is done around them. People who have an extremely high need for control over others are considered as control freaks.

Their main attempt is to hide their vulnerabilities by ensuring that everything within their surroundings is under their control. They try hard to manipulate people and put so much pressure on them just so that they don't have to change themselves. Everywhere you go, you will spot a control freak – whether at home, school, or workplace.

With the right strategies up your sleeve, you can deal with them and live a happy life.

Get rid of turf wars

So many control freaks often feel the need to retain control of each aspect of their work just because they do not want to lose their status. It could be that there was a time when they were the only employee in the office and were used to doing all things by themselves. The problem with these kinds of people is the fact that they are very difficult to handle because of their resistance to change – especially growth and expansion.

The real problem is that they feel that the person who has just joined the workplace is out to get "their" job. At first, they did not need any help, and now, they still think that they don't need any help whatsoever. It does not matter how competent the other person is because the control freak will not welcome any ideas or suggestions that are not theirs.

To deal with such a person; what you need to do is get rid of turf wars by ensuring that you engage them fully during role allocation. Allow them to create their projects so that they feel as though they have a sense of tenure. If it is possible, you can separate their duties from those of other employees. Once they see that their roles are highly valuable to the company, they will ease off on their controlling attitude – giving the others ample space and time to go about their duties with minimal interruptions.

Stroke their ego

According to research, there is evidence that shows control freaks are often very insecure. The thing with such people is that they often fight just so that they can retain control, considering that they are not sure of themselves. Such people hate trying new things and desperately are afraid of new situations and events. They feel that by retaining control over their work surrounding – something familiar to them – they can keep their insecurities in check.

Well, unfortunately, the approach they use in controlling things and people around them depicts their domineering and overbearing attitudes. This is precisely what stands to undermine their self-esteem and confidence further – especially if they spent the time to evaluate their behaviors honestly.

To deal with such kind of people, you need to find a way to help them regain their control so that they can feel secure. The best way to do this is for you to appeal to their ego. While they may come off as confident people, the truth is that inside, they are fragile. They are just hiding under that assertive shell so that they can win others' approval. Before they can offer you any help, go to them and ask them to help you with a difficult task. Even when you feel as though things are not looking up, simply compliment them on anything so that they can relax and make it easier for them to relinquish control over small things.

Stand your ground

There are instances when you feel that there is nothing you can do to appease someone who is controlling. This is because they firmly believe that they know best. They will even go as far as throwing tantrums if they don't get their way.

The best way to handle them is to try and assess what it is that you disagree on. If it is something important, you should stand your ground. While this may stir up conflict and friction at the workplace, it will help them know that not everyone can toy around. The trick is that you choose your battles with caution. If it is an issue of how the office should be cleaned, ask yourself whether it is something you would want to die for.

Take note of the little things

Just like stroking their ego, taking note of small things is about paying attention to what their needs are. Whatever it is, ensure that you pay attention to these tendencies. Reassure them that they are doing an incredible job. Tell them that the place would not be as excellent as it is without them. Praise them for their underlying qualities, and before long, you will realize that their controlling attitude reduces significantly as they soak in praise!

Give a little

Is there someone in your office or home that thinks they know so much more than anyone else? Does it even matter that they believe this? Well, the truth is that in the grand scheme of things, the question that truly matters is if this person is involved in all your daily activities and your ability to do your job. If they don't stand in the way of you getting your job done, the best way to tame them would be to give to her selfish and immature attitude – and simply move on.

Ask questions

One thing you will note about a control freak is that they often are obnoxious. Several people around them dismiss them because of their bossy attitude and desire to control every little thing. Well, the truth is that in reality, they just desire to be part of something – and can offer valuable input – if only people would listen.

Therefore, the next time you encounter a control freak at home or in the office, and they want to boss you around, ask them pointed questions about how they want this or that to be done. If they insist on installing the lights in a specific manner, ask them why they think it cannot be done differently. It could be that they have a phobia for heights, and that is why they insist that it be done a different way than that avoids falling. This allows you to realize that these control issues do not hurt and have the potential of affecting their security in the workplace or at home.

If they are adamant that stationeries go to the right side of their desk and then picture frames on the left, demand for an explanation, there are times when you will realize that they don't have a valid reason for that. If it is not their desk, then that is unacceptable. However, if it is their desk, the best thing is for you to oblige. The point is for you to help them confront their obsessions so that you can know whether there is an actual control issue going on or there is something else subtler that goes beyond stationeries.

Spending time with them talking about these issues will help both of you resolve the problems amicably so that you can both get back to what matters and be productive at it.

If necessary, enlist the help

What if you are not able to reach a point of compromise with someone who is a control freak? In such a case, you can seek advice from your superiors or line manager. You must try to explain to them that your intention is not to cause disharmony in the office. Instead, what you are interested in is creating an atmosphere where each one of you can thrive.

This will also go a long way in helping the boss understand that you are not there to complain but that you have the company's best interest at heart. You must tell your manager that the other person's tendencies are getting in the way of you working and reaching your goals. Ask them to clarify what your roles and responsibilities are at the office. There is a chance that the management has no idea of what the situation is like, and asking them to step in will help a great deal to clear things up.

It is also essential that you are always ready to offer possible solutions to the issue so that your bosses are aware that you are also a team player. While working with someone who is controlling can be difficult, realize that it does not have to be impossible! Just a little effort aimed at understanding their motivations and alleviating their insecurities will go a long way in helping you work together in harmony.

Narcissists

Narcissists are people who are ready challenging to work mainly because of their big ego and vanity. The problem with them is that they pretend to know it all. If you have such a person at home or the workplace, you must determine where they are real experts and where they are pretentious.

If they are real experts, then your research should prove that they are knowledgeable in that area because of the validity of their ideas and information. You must not subjugate their ideas or permit any condescension. The trick is for you to be respectful when dealing with them. Where you feel they are wrong, simply correct them without being confrontational or overly aggressive.

Gossips

With the advent of technological devices, gossiping is no longer restricted to the water cooler. Today, people gossip with ease of emails and social media platforms. What is interesting is that in spite of all these technological innovations, chatting today at the office or home can be traced back to one single individual who always knows and shares information – whether true or false.

If you have such a person in your life, the best way to deal with them is to avoid sharing information with them or someone close to them. You must practice remaining cordial when around them. Whenever they try to pry into your life or that of others, gently pull away from the conversation and change the subject into something more productive and useful.

Bullies

These people are a fact of life, and the most unfortunate thing is that by the time they are graduating high school, if they will not have changed, then chances are that they will never change. These are the kind of people who end up taking their insecurities to the workplace, marriages, and friendships. The problem is thinking of others as weak and susceptible and hence use that to be vindictive. They will always try to get other people to gang up against one or more people around them.

When you are dealing with such a person, you must try as much as you can to hide your weaknesses. Stand up to them, and don't tolerate them being respectful to you. Don't get me wrong; I don't mean that you get aggressive with them. However, you must not allow them to interfere with your life. If they try to bring their attitude to your place of work or home, simply ask them to leave.

Slackers

These are the kind of people who are not motivated and are unreliable. They are the kind that cannot carry their weight. If you have never worked with one of these, thank you, God! They are the kind of people who will leave all the work to you. When you are asked to partner with them, ensure that the job assigned to them is done to completion. If not, then you should be prepared to take on their portion of work.

Trust me; they are out there to let people down – beware!

Pessimists

Some people view the world through shades of gray. They are the pessimists whose primary agenda is to dismiss every idea someone comes up with without necessarily offering an alternative. Much of their time is spent complaining about this or that. If you have such a person in your team, the trick is to remain positive.

Remind them that you cannot just sit and do nothing; instead, they should give their contributions as well.

Oh, and be prepared to shoulder much of the work!

The hostile or bossy

The one thing I have learned when dealing with these kinds of people is that strength and tact goes a long way. People who feel as though they have been wronged tend to be violent.

The other trick is for you to try as much as you can to help them meet their needs without necessarily being aggressive or discriminatory about it. Try to stay away from any interaction with them that stirs up intense emotions like violence – as they say, don't hang out with the enemy when they are carrying a weapon or drinking! Check your actions to ensure that they don't stir up anger. In short, try not to be a pushover.

The worst thing you can do is strongly retaliate against an aggressive person. Remember that hostility often begets hostility. The best thing you can do is try to divert their attention to something more meaningful. This way, their anger tends to go down. Try to explain to them more about the situation pointing out common interests so that they are open to calm and rational ways of resolving the issue at hand.

The chronic complainer

These are the kind of people who will always find fault in everything you do. They will go to the extent of blaming you. They pretend as though they know all that should be done when, in fact, they are never open to correcting the situation themselves in the first place.

If you want to cope with these kinds of people, the first thing is for you to pay attention to all they have to say and then ask questions to seek clarification — even though you have been falsely accused or are guilty. The secret is for you not to complain, apologize, or be overly-defensive. If you do, then you are causing them to restate their concerns in a more heated manner. You must be severe and supportive of it. Accept the facts and get all the complaints in writing. Involve them in the process so that you all actively find the solution. Rather than dwelling too much on what is wrong, try to get them to think of what should be done.

The Super-Agreeable

Has anyone ever agreed with everything and anything you say to the point that they make you angry? Well, these are the super-agreeable people. While it is a good thing to get along with people at home and the workplace, some people agree with every idea you give, and then when things suddenly go south; they back down.

What you need to note about these people is that they are after approval. We all come from different family backgrounds with diverse upbringings. Some learned that the best way to get love is through pretense. In the same way, those people who are super-agreeable tend to promise heaven on earth but cannot deliver that. They will tell you, "I will submit the report tomorrow, or I will help you run errands." Don't be fooled; all they are doing is buttering you up.

The best way to handle them is to assure them that it is okay to say "No" when they feel like they will not be able to deliver. It is okay to speak the truth even when it is hard to spit it out. You must take time to ask them to try and be candid so that they can find it easy to come out and be frank about anything. When you support them overcome this habit, they will stop making promises they know they couldn't possibly keep. Show them that you value the relationship you have, and the truth won't hurt. Ensure that you let them know you are ready to compromise, considering that they will be fair and just.

Critics

Criticism is not all that bad, but the truth is that there are times and places for it. Debates are where the most effective solutions are birth. This is where some of the best minds challenge every point of view in the room.

But is that always the case with criticism? Are there demanding critics?

Indeed, there are so many demanding critics whose criticism is destructive. They are not seeking answers. They are not even concerned with the give and take that leads to a strong team and a consensus. They are the people who behave like politicians. I like to think of critics as spectators and not players.

Look around your office; is there is a critic there? Is your spouse or friend a critic?

Often, you will notice that critics are the kind of people who will always be quick to point a finger, and yet when their help is needed, they will not lift one. They are the kind of people who will not cooperate within the project, and it is their negative attitude that makes it hard to work and achieve the set goals in a team.

Chapter 4: Employees Who Blame Others

Who they are: A common employee problem is caused by those members of the team who refuse to take responsibility for their own actions. If ever something goes wrong, it is always somebody else's fault. We're not talking here about an employee who usually does a good job but happens to raise issues with other people once or twice. We're talking about a member of staff that blames others repeatedly, in fact almost every single time that you raise issues with their work. They may try to throw the blame back onto you – claiming your instructions were unclear, your directions were flawed or you didn't give them enough time – or they may even try to blame their fellow workmates. Perhaps X didn't do Y in time for him or her to do Z.

What to do: It's often hard to deal with an employee who specialises in throwing the blame around because they always seem to have an excuse or an answer for everything. The key, however, is not to get caught up in their justifications.

Don't start arguing about who really did what or allow yourself to get backed into a corner where you need to defend your actions. Instead, keep the emphasis on them; stress that they need to take responsibility when things aren't done on time. Don't allow them to throw the issues back at you. Listen to everything they say and then ask yourself the key question - did they take ownership of the issue or take responsibility? If they didn't, they're simply blaming others. There's always something that an employee could have done to rectify any situation, even if it just includes coming to you for help earlier.

Point out that you would expect the employee to deal with any roadblocks in the way of the project personally; emphasise that if they don't have the seniority needed to do so, they should come to you as soon as the problem arises. Chances are that these alleged barriers don't really exist but by offering to help, you remove their ability to use it as an excuse for shoddy work.

Be firm; don't cave in at the first sign of aggression or tears (you may get either or both). Stick to the issue and refuse to be waylaid by the excuses they throw at you. Look at our sample conversation for guidance on how to do that. If the problem persists, you may have to level with them and say the immortal words, 'Don't blame other people.'

There is a school of thought that those people with social disorders are more likely to blame others; it is also closely linked to bipolar disorder. If you manage such people, you may want to take specialist expert advice on how to handle this.

In the meantime, however, make it clear to the employee that you will not accept or give in to the blame game. This is much easier to do if you have a non-blame game culture in your working environment.

What do I mean by a blame-game culture? Well, let's be honest: we've all worked for bosses that are all too ready to take the credit for any work well done but to pass the blame onto others for any mistakes. This sets up a culture of blame across the department.

A boss should never pass the blame or look for someone to censure to get themself off the hook; as the boss, you hired and manage all the people who work under you, so, ultimately, the buck stops with you. That doesn't mean that you can't work with individual members of staff to raise their game if need be, but don't give in to the blame culture. You will never earn the respect of your employees that way. This is especially true if someone from another department complains about your team; as the manager, you should always accept the blame on you and the department as a whole, rather than singling out individual employees.

Of course, sometimes when people point out flaws with other employees, the issues could be genuine. That's not really what we're talking about here; in this section, we're talking about someone who has a pathological need to blame others to take the responsibility away from themselves. If a trusted employee raises issues, on the other hand, you need to investigate those as you would any other concerns with your team.

In addition, let employees know that it is ok to make mistakes as long as they learn from them; it's the only real way they can work without fear and have the confidence and creativity to try new things.

So before you take the employee to task for passing the blame, make sure you stamp it out across the board and lead by example. Once you have, make sure the employee knows passing the buck or the blame will not be tolerated again.

Here's an example of how that conversation could go:

Manager: "Hello Janet. I've asked you for a chat today to talk about the Dyer project. As you know, the project came in late and had to be significantly redone before we could pass it to the client; as someone who was in charge of the project, I wanted to ask you what you thought had gone wrong?"

Employee: "I'm glad you asked. There were a few problems with the project. I was trying my best to keep it on track but, to be honest, I found John's work a bit sloppy and I had to spend all my time correcting him. I then didn't have enough time to do my own; I asked Sue and Alan for help but they wouldn't co-operate with me. It would have been fine if they had stepped up."

Manager: "I see. And what steps did you take to control the situation?"

Employee; "Well I asked them to co-operate with me but they wouldn't."

Manager: "Well, you were in charge of the project so let's not blame others. What steps did you take to rectify the problem?"

Employee: "They wouldn't help."

Manager: "I want to concentrate on what you could have done to control the situation. What other actions did you take to solve the problem?"

Employee: "Well, because Sue and Alan wouldn't help me, there wasn't...."

Manager: "Janet, I want to have a conversation about your actions, not anyone else's. Mistakes are allowed in this company as long as we learn from them. As you were in charge of the project, you are responsible for its success and if something doesn't work out, we need to discuss how we can prevent the problem in the future. Now, I think it would be better if you come forward and tell me if there's a problem with any project in the future so that we can deal with it nice and early, don't you?"

Employee: "Yes, ok, but if people don't do their work on time or refuse to help me, what can I do?" *

Manager: "Janet, stop! The only way you will get into trouble now is if you continue to make excuses or blame other people. Let's have an honest, open discussion about what went wrong today, ok? This actually brings up some behaviour that I want to talk to you about…"

* As an aside, let's spend a quick moment answering this question as if it were genuine: there will be cases in your managerial career where blame may be justified (but it equally may not, that's what you need to find out). So how should you deal with that? The first thing to stress again is that you don't want a blame culture at work; you do, however, need to address the issue to find out what went wrong and how the team can learn from it in the future.

The best thing to do is to get all the relevant people around a table in a private room and try to get to the bottom of what went wrong. Don't make it about criticism but point out that the project wasn't done to standard and you want to find out why that was. Open the floor up to anyone and ask them what, if anything, caused problems. You may well find out that there was a bottleneck with one person, as alleged, BUT it could be that there was a genuine reason for it, such as overwork, poor resources or insufficient knowledge.

Keep a white board or a written record of the complaints as they come in to help you stay on track; it's easy to be distracted from your main aim when everyone is talking and conversation is moving on. Don't allow the meeting to become a lynch mob or for it to descend into a list of moans about the company or working practices.

Keep the meeting focused, always bring it back to how the issues could be prevented in the future and come up with a plan for a better way of working on the back of their observations if you consider them genuine. It could be as simple as formulating a way to alert others to the status of the work earlier or reminding someone that they need to help out now and again. If the meeting highlights specific problems with an individual's work that need to be addressed over and above your new processes, take note of it but don't address it in front of other people. Speak to that employee in private afterwards.

Chapter 5: Identify With The Difficult Person

Okay, now we know what is making this person so miserable that he/she cannot help but to make everyone else feel his or her pain. What is the old saying? Misery loves company. Now you might say, "This does not give a person the right to rain down their misery on others." And you will be 100% correct. There is nothing that gives anyone the right to do this to another; but it still happens. And what can we do about it?

The first thing that you can do to understand why this person is unhappy is to put yourself in this person's shoes. How would you feel if your mother was dying of cancer, and you had to come to work every day because you have no one else to pay your bills? How would you feel if you had a disease that caused you pain every day? How would you feel if your husband just walked out on you and left you with three children to raise? Again, do these things give them the right to rain on your parade? No, they don't. But can you be a little more tolerant if you understand why this person is not perky and smiling? Sure, you can.

By putting yourself in another person's place, you can now see how an unplanned snap or comment can come out of one's mouth without much thought. You can see how insignificant your hurt feelings are compared to the major issues that another human being is dealing with—and to them, they might seem like insurmountable problems.

Instead of snapping back at this person and causing them more grief, or going to your boss and reporting this person, how else can you handle this situation? A little bit of compassion can go a long way in building on a good working relationship with this person.

Respect this person's privacy, but if they are willing to share their situation with you, be a good listener. Offer to do anything you can do to help them—even if it is just helping them with their job duties. Just letting another person know that you respect them and are willing to help, can make them aware that how they treated you was wrong, and they will probably apologize to you. And always be gracious when you get an apology. Remember, you could be this person sometime.

After you have identified with this person, put yourself in this person's shoes, what else can you do to try to create a better working relationship with the difficult person?

Chapter 6: Let's Define Difficult People

Human relationships are the foundation of the society. People find mutual interests and values which transform into shared goals, paving the way to established associations, economic alliances, educational institutions to name a few. It is by working together that society turns the wheel of progress. This is even truer today with the world being easily interconnected through the internet.

Due to this nature of people, we find ourselves constantly faced with different personalities, attitudes and behaviors. To be an effective person, we must always be the force that brings out the best in people. However, inevitably, we will meet people who are difficult to deal with in various situations: may it be at work, at home or in public. How we handle the situation is critical because relationships are the threads to the fabric of society.

There are different types of people who incite enmity in us, from feelings of annoyance, irritation, anger or distrust. Identifying what particular attitude it is that bothers us will help us understand how to deal with them.

People Pleaser

You may wonder why a people pleaser is someone who is difficult to deal with. Sure enough, he tries his best to be nice to everyone and to be the superhero that helps everyone with their deadlines. However, he also can't say no and he has difficulty giving crucial criticisms. He would rather be everybody's favorite than tell the truth.

The first encounter wouldn't reveal any problems. In fact, you'd think you've met the kindest, warmest and best person in the world. But as you get to know the person more, you will begin to doubt whether he is giving any helpful input at all or if he can really deliver on his commitments because you realize that the People Pleaser just tells you what you want to hear.

The Bull

Characterized with a mean aggressive personality, The Bull is someone who is immediately demanding, always wants to get their way and doesn't listen to others' opinion. Although no one appointed him boss or leader, he just feels the need to steer the group in the direction he feels you should take, regardless of what anyone else thinks.

The Bull gets things done for sure. But he does this by either whipping up a whirlwind solution or by bullying people into making things happen. He creates an intimidating environment that will make most people shy away and clam up in their shells.

Invisible Man

Another person who's difficult to deal with is one who is always absent and doesn't participate or give any inputs. In every group, there is always someone who just gets swept into the flurry of activity. He has perfected the appearance of being part of the group, sharing the responsibilities and free-riding on the credit. On the other hand, the group also gives him tasks that are also assigned to another person, just in case. He plays a back-up role that you're sure will never be needed. To put it simply, he's a redundant member of the group and deadweight.

The Pessimist

With a dark cloud overhead that he brings everywhere, the pessimist comes in with a heavy feeling. He never fails to see a negative angle in every situation. He doesn't believe in positive thinking and just can't seem to find any reason to go on living.

The Pessimist is difficult to deal with especially in high-pressure situations when everyone just tries to lighten up. Being friends with this type of person would also oblige you to constantly supply him with words of inspiration, motivation and kindness. But ultimately, all efforts go to waste as they seem to just go into a black hole that can never be filled.

The Whiner

While everyone experiences hard times and problems, The Whiner just can't seem to talk about anything else. Understandably, talking things out and venting is a good outlet for negative feelings and will help one get over his problems. That's perfectly fine, for as long as one actually passes on to something else.

Whiners, however, just complain about everything from the big things to the littlest of things. This is a chronic behavior and overtakes his entire life.

The Baby

Babies are adorably cute, but having to constantly take care of them, especially if they're not even helpless anymore, are difficult. The Baby is entirely dependent on the people around him. He cannot assume responsibility or make decisions for himself, much less the work or people around him. He needs 24/7 supervision in his work and affirmation that he is doing the right thing every step of the way.

The VIP

The whole world revolves around the VIP, and he expects everybody else to know that gravity has shifted. He is the center of attention. All conversations must be about him or must include him. No problem or achievement is greater than his. No one is better than he is. His word is the law.

These are just some of the rules that are implemented in his world.

Chapter 7: Overcoming Evil With Good

This chapter is based on how to overcome negativity using positivity. One of the ways to get along with a difficult person is learn how to be good at all times.

When a difficult, furious or unmerciful boss at work or a superior see that no matter the gravity of evil or wickedness he /she is perpetrating and the receiver seems to adjust, and adjust, adjust without reacting back, he or she will calm down and come down.

Difficult people often have the traces of egotism in them. They feel bigger than they are, they will always demand respect even if they really don't worth it. And they don't like being rude to. They hate any form of objection and they expect all orders to be followed strictly.

When one is in this type of situation and he/she has no other choice than to concur, then he/she must learn how to overcome evil with goodness.

No matter how hard a heart is, no matter how difficult someone proves to be, he can always be overpowered by being good to him.

Two wrongs cannot make a right. You can't fight problems with more problems. You can't quench fire using more fire. The best way to kill a bacterial is to apply anti-bacterial. Evil can never overcome evil. Only goodness can overcome evil. This is why you must be careful and be able to win anyone with the power of goodness no matter what.

How do you overcome a difficult mind with goodness?

Maintain your cool and gentleness, come what may.

Follow orders strictly if it is a must, especially in the place of work. (If you are in a relationship with difficult person, and you are yet to get married, after much pleasing and trying to overcome him/her with goodness from your side but the person seems not to change, the best advice is to back out. Love is not selfish and neither is it easily puffed up. If your love in the person's heart can't quench the fire of being difficult combined with your kindness, then you must run for your life. A broken relationship is better than a broken marriage. A person that refuses to change towards you during courtship will never or find it hard to change in marriage.

Same applies to friendship too. If the other party isn't considering the value of your friendship and the goodness you have exhibited, then you can apply this type of goodness which is to; decrease the closeness and tightness. In this type of situation, you master the habit of not being too close or far.

Prayer

The only army that fight on their knees are Christians. Prayer is the strongest and most potent invisible weapon anyone can wield. No battle is too hard for prayer to overcome. No mind or heart can be so stubborn for prayers to handle.

 When you are facing person or you have to deal with him, and after you have tried all your possible best, nothing seems to change, the best thing to do is to report such heart to its maker and source. And that is God. The Bible says the hearts of kings are in the hands of the Lord. The hearts of all men are in the hands of the Almighty, and he can turn them wherever He wishes or change them to please His own people.

A hard can become very soft and penetrable when God has intervened.

There was a time I needed to discuss certain things with a difficult lecturer while I was on campus. I knew fully well that the man was a difficult type and he hardly give students audience after class. And hardly will a student be allowed to enter his office to pour out his or her mind.

After I've made up my mind to go, I went to God in prayer; I put his heart in to God's hands and I asked God to soften his heart for me. So that he could listen to me and entertain my discussion.

After waiting on God for three days, I went to his office and to my surprise, it seems he was in a good mood that moment. It seemed as if he had just received a good news. He gave me the audience I needed and attended to my case. I understood it was God at work and not just coincidence.

So, if you must deal with someone who Is difficult, either a superior, a boss, a husband or a wife, a father or a mother, try applying prayer after trying your best. Talk to their creator the owner if the hearts of all men.

Chapter 8: How To Deal With A Needy Person

Having to live with a needy person is really quite a challenge. The Leech always wants your time and attention and always needs your perpetual assurance to be happy and contented. Yes, it can be extremely annoying, frustrating, and exhausting being with a dependent person, and it will take a lot of your tolerance and fortitude to deal with one. Assuming that the difficult person is close to you and you can't simple avoid her, here are some practical tips to help you maintain your own emotional wellbeing when you have a needy loved one.

1. Clarify each other's expectations

Sit down and talk about the expectations you have for each other. Explain that you are not her savior and you cannot be there to take care of her all the time so she needs to learn how to take care of herself. Make it clear that you also want her to experience personal growth that will actually be beneficial for her in the long run. Talk about the probable great outcomes.

2. Express your feelings and be honest

There is really something about telling the truth when building a long term relationship. You are not helping your loved one if you constantly lie to her just to avoid hurting her and tolerate her neediness. In cases when you weren't able to do what she had requested, lovingly tell her the real reason why you haven't done so. Explain to her that she needs to learn how to do things on her own and to not depend on you too much. Make her realize that you both need some level of independence to be able to function well in society. Of course, tell her these things with much love as possible. You can start by saying, "You know how much I love you, but..." Tell her how you really feel about her being very clingy.

3. Modify your approach

Change the way you talk to her and the manner you address her with the intention of boosting her self-esteem. A needy person is insecure and has low self-confidence, and this can be improved by making her realize that she is strong and capable. All of this starts by how you treat her. If you treat her like a baby, then she will indeed act like one. If you treat her as someone you can count on, then she will learn how to become responsible and mature.

4. Encourage individuality

Support her to spend time alone or create her own schedule. Give her the opportunity to do a few things by herself. Washing her clothes or dishes can be a great start. Do not always be there when she needs you and help her help herself. Let her get used to some minor inconveniences. Teach her how to handle disappointments and how to let go of unrealistic expectations.

5. Introduce a sense of interdependence

Make her realize through your example that what you both need is interdependence, not independence or dependence. Show her that it is possible to work as a team and help each other out without being a burden to the other person. When one person is in trouble, the other person is able to assist, and vice versa. By establishing this kind of relationship, both of you will be better and more satisfied. You can avoid the feeling of always being the dominant partner and she can improve her self-esteem all at the same time.

Chapter 9: Play More Nicely

When dealing with a difficult person, you usually feel like you are alone. You are standing on one side of a fence, and he or she is standing on the other side. It may seem practically impossible to hop the fence and work out differences. However, you would be surprised how much easier difficult interactions with people become when you extend your hand metaphorically and try to work with them as a team.

There are many different ways to work with people to resolve difficult situations and conflicts. Sometimes, just talking about it helps. Communication is always essential for conflict resolution. Becoming a better communicator is crucial to removing the blockages that prevent easy human interaction. The keys to good communication are nestled in this chapter.

Facilitate a Team Effort

Facilitating a team effort is when you make it appear like you are actively working with someone on a solution. You are a pair, or a team. But how can you invoke this feeling in people?

The first step is to have a solution-oriented attitude. Show this to others by asking questions like, "How can I make this better?" Really show your interest in reaching a solution. By expressing this interest to the other person, you are basically extending an offer of help while inviting him or her to join you in the endeavor.

The second step is to actively make an effort to accomplish a reasonable solution with someone. You can't just say you want to help and then not help. This is an actual effort that you must make. When the other person sees you making this effort, he or she will more than likely jump in as well. Actively talk or search for a solution to the problem that is causing someone to be difficult to you.

It is important to not be overbearing in this endeavor. This is not all about you. It is also about the other person. Focus on him or her and what he or she says. Do not become bossy, or you will just cause yet more resentment and conflict.

Be open to things like compromise. Also be open to using persuasion, which is covered in more depth in Chapter 7. A difficult person is a puzzle that you must do anything to peacefully work around and placate. You must open yourself up to a wide variety of solutions and never give up until you find the best one.

"We" speech is helpful in teamwork. Say a lot of "we" terms to make the other person feel like he or she is included in your thinking. This will subconsciously trigger someone to feel like you are on the same team. In fact, it can be helpful to use "we" terms right off the bat with anyone to create a cooperative teamwork bond from the start. A lot of friction can be shed if you approach people like teammates and try to work with them, instead of against them.

It is perfectly acceptable to want to be superior at times. Especially if you are very knowledgeable in a certain field or subject, you can be superior. But understand that having a condescending attitude is a surefire way to alienate other people. People will not like you or want to work with you if you appear to be a know-it-all. Instead, have an open mind and accept new information. Even if you already know everything about something, smile and thank people for their expertise. You will find that people will respect you much more if you do not tout your infinite knowledge all of the time.

You also should never be accusing when you are trying to work with people. It is easy and natural to become resentful of certain people. You may want to say things like, "Because of you, this happened" or "Thanks for ruining my day." But it is important to not hold this attitude if you want to avoid further conflict. Instead, dissolve your resentment with a sense of humor. Do not level accusations or unkind statements at other people, or they will just get defensive. Say that you do not like the conflict and that you want to work things out. Never implicate someone's fault in any situation, no matter how big or how small.

People also tend to love solid, basic ideas and plain language. Making things less complicated is a good way to open communication with other people. Try to end conflict and make someone feel included in your efforts by eliminating confusing or unnecessarily fancy communication from your dialogue. While big words are a sign of intelligence, people will actually appreciate it if you use simpler language. They will feel like you are trying your best to be clear and direct, which will make them feel like a part of the team.

Finally, never be afraid to take the lead. Every team needs a leader, even if it is just a two-person team trying to overcome a conflict. If you are trying to create a conflict resolution team of some sort with at least one other person, you can appoint yourself the leader by taking the initiative. If you do not take this initiative, then the other person probably will not either. You two will get nowhere as a result. Do not be afraid to be the bigger person and start the team effort on your own. Other people will respect this and follow your lead.

Communicate Better

You already saw how important communication is for dealing with difficult people. I have mentioned opening good communication in almost every section of this book for good reason. A great deal of difficult situations with people arise over misunderstandings and poor communication. Having great communication skills can also help you resolve conflicts with people by searching out and targeting their needs and making it clear that you want to help, not fight. You would be surprised at how much difficult people will soften and work with you when you begin practicing good communication skills.

Many people believe that they are great communicators. They blame difficult situations and miscommunication on circumstances or other people, not themselves. But if you are running into difficult people frequently, you may want to reevaluate your communication skills. Let's put it this way. You can never be too good at communicating with other people. NLP Tips for Great Communication

Neuro-linguistic programming (NLP) is basically a philosophy or lifestyle that teaches you to use the neurological, linguistic, and physical attributes of yourself or other people to achieve your ideal results. While it can be used for a plethora of means, possibly the most beneficial aspect of NLP is learning how to communicate most effectively with other people.

Intentions

In order to be a great communicator, you need to set a very clear intention for your communication. If you do not understand your own intention, then your listener certainly won't. You want to know exactly what you want to communicate. You also need to know your desired outcome for an interaction. For example, if you are confronting a very difficult co-worker about her obnoxious and unfeeling behavior, you need to set some intentions and desired outcomes for the confrontation. You may want to set the intention of helping this co-worker adjust her behavior so that you get along better with her. You may also want to express your feelings, which she has hurt. Your desired outcome is having a more peaceful and less hurtful relationship with this co-worker, so that you can complete your job without wanting to strangle her or to lock yourself in the restroom and cry.

Plan out conversations with difficult people before you initiate the conversation in reality. Envision how you want the conversation to go. Imagine how the person you are talking to will respond to you. Make a goal for what you want to achieve with the communication. The more you do this, the clearer your communication will become. You can avoid pesky misunderstandings because you do not make the mistake of being unintentionally vague.

Sensory Acuity

NLP believes that all people have a preferred sensory acuity, or perceptive sense. Some people prefer auditory, while others prefer visual, and yet others prefer gustatory, olfactory, or tactile. You can gather clues about what sensory acuity people prefer from their speech. A tactile person will say stuff like, "I love how that feels" and "Do you feel what I'm saying?" A more visual person will utter phrases like, "Do you see what I mean?" and "That looks really nice." Auditory people will refer to hearing, olfactory people to smell, and gustatory people to taste.

Now it is very important to find someone's sensory preference because you can use that information to facilitate smoother communication. People will respond to you better if you use their preferred sensory acuity when you speak to them. For instance, if you are an auditory person but you gather that a person that you are talking to is more visual, start using visual references in your speech, such as, "Do you see what I am saying?"

Matching

Matching is another NLP tip for getting people to communicate well with you. Match someone's breathing to give him or her a sense of being close to you. Matching your breathing rate to that of a difficult person can make him or her suddenly like you and respond to you better.

Matching facial expressions and body movements is also helpful. People find comfort in similarity. They will like you more if you seem similar to them.

Finding common ground with someone is also helpful. Imagine that you are dealing with a very difficult customer who is shouting at your co-workers. You can instantly appease her temper by pointing out that you like her earrings and you have a similar pair yourself that you wear often. Or if a difficult family member likes a certain sport, try to get into the sport with him. Watch how quickly people simmer down when they see that you share common interests with them.

Tonality

There is a lot more to communication than just words. In the next section, I will talk about body language. But tonality is also a big part of communication. Tonality is how you phrase words and the tone and volume of voice that you use. In fact, an estimated thirty-eight percent of communication lies in how you say things. It isn't what you say, it's how you say it.

Use more positive terms when you are dealing with a pessimistic or doubtful person. For instance, describe a car as "fast, efficient, and attractive." Don't say things like, "That car won't leave you stranded on the side of the road." Even though that statement may seem positive, it is really negative because you are talking about a potential negative event. Avoid bringing up negative events or using terms like "won't," "don't," and "can't."

Also use subtler language. Instead of using strong words like "steal," use the more lax word "take." This lessens the drama and seriousness of the conversation for others, so that they feel more comfortable talking to you.

Keep the volume of your voice reasonable. Never raise your voice when dealing with a difficult person, or you will probably set yourself up for communication failure. Use a gentler, more soothing voice when dealing with upset people to calm them down. You can raise the intonation at the end of sentences if you want to appear more approachable. Alternatively, you can lower your voice if you want to appear more competent and intelligent.

Body Language

The nonverbal aspects of communication account for fifty-five percent of your communication. The way you posture your body as you speak tells others a lot that you do not say. Conversely, you can gather a lot of information from how others posture and carry themselves as they speak to you. You need to be very aware and mindful of your own physiology, as well as others'.

You want to be as open as possible when you talk to other people, particularly difficult people. Around rude or unpleasant people, you naturally will desire to cross your arms and brace yourself against them. But it is better to have a relaxed, neutral posture when you speak to others. Relax your arms at your sides and lower your shoulders.

Eye contact is also crucial. You do not want to stare into someone's eyes during normal conversation or conflict resolution, but you also do not want to avoid making eye contact. Eye contact lets others know that you are sincere and that you can be trusted. Relax and try to meet someone's eyes often.

When dealing with difficult people, you may find that mirroring is helpful. This is when you mimic some of the motions that someone makes while talking. If someone leans toward you, you can take a brief three-second pause and then lean toward him or her as well. Mirroring makes others like you more since they recognize similarities in you.

You should always have a confident posture, with your shoulders back, spine straight, and head held high. This posture lets others know that you cannot be bullied. It also lets them know that you are a knowledgeable and authoritative person, so they will want to listen to you. Managers are usually great at adopting this posture and using firm language to settle disputes with unhappy or inappropriate customers. Model your behavior after these managers and do not ever give in.

Behavior Patterns

People communicate a lot with their physiology and tonality. Observe and interact with behavior patterns that other people exhibit during communication. When you do this, you become more sensitive to what others are saying without speaking out loud. People will appreciate it when you pick up on their subtle cues, without forcing them to speak about something directly. Speaking directly can be awkward and even rude, so do not force people to spell things out for you. Gather and respond to their behavioral hints before they have to say something out loud.

Watch for external shifts in behavior when you are communicating. Facial expressions may change ever so slightly. Someone may cross his or her arms in defensiveness, or may shift slightly toward an exit, indicating discomfort. When someone's cheeks flush, he or she is feeling more heated emotion and getting more excited. When you notice a change in someone's tonality or volume of voice, you can surmise that his or her emotions have changed and a topic is important to him or her.

Always respond to someone's behavioral patterns during communication. Not doing so can make you seem stubborn, insensitive, careless, or even unintelligent. If someone tries to express emotion through behavior, try your best to placate negative emotions and encourage positive emotions. Offer your coat if someone shivers or offer to talk somewhere else if someone shifts subtly toward the exit. Read customers to gauge their concerns about the products or services that you are selling. Doing these little things can make a world of difference because it makes others feel like you actually care.

Chapter 10: Easy Rules Of Dealing With Difficult People

When dealing with difficult people, your reputation is also on the line. What you door say might affect your good name. Your mental and emotional health may also be affected. Here are some simple rules to keep in mind when you encounter difficult people.

Think before you act

Before you respond or do anything, give it a thought and try to predict the likely outcome of such a response. In this way, you'll be avoiding unpleasant situations. If you react abruptly without thinking, you may have to deal with the consequences that may arise. You don't want this burden. When you give a well thought our response, either verbally or by your actions you get that other person to think as well.

Keep your cool

In every situation, always keep your cool, no matter how bad the other person reacts; don't let them get to your head. Nobody has the power to control your temper unless you let them. Keeping your cool disarms the other person since they would be looking for a confrontation and also enables you to think through the best course of action. We have seen people lose their cool in a traffic situation and ending up doing something regrettable. Sure there will be some challenging people who'll stretch your patience but never lose your cool.

Don't take it personally

When you encounter a difficult person always keep in mind that what they are expressing on the outside is just a reflection of their inner turmoil. It's not about you at all, it's about them. Someone might be going through a hard time in their life and are bound to get easily get triggered to anger. The best you should do is to understand them and try helping them deal with the issue at hand in a different way. When someone sees you care about them and empathize with them, they are bound to change their attitude towards you.

Search within

In some situations, a person gets difficult as a reaction to your attitude or behavior. So before you blame or judge, first check within to find out if your attitude is right. This is something difficult to do as most people tend to think that they are not the problem. You might have offended someone even unintentionally. If you find out you might be the cause of different attitude you are experiencing from those close to you, make it a point to resolve the issues. When you do this in a timely manner, you avoid any buildup of bitterness and animosity.

Know your goal

In anything we do we have something we want to achieve, even in our conversations. When you understand what your goal is, you rise above all other petty issues that are normally the cause of difficult interactions with others. You won't seek revenge, neither will you wish to cause any harm to another person.

Listen actively

Most of the arguments we have are brought about by lack of listening. If people employed active listening skills, most conflicts would be avoided. Listen with the intention to understand rather than to respond. Misunderstandings fuel conflicts which can make working with people very difficult. Once you have understood what the other person means both by the verbal and nonverbal communication, you are in a good place to give an appropriate response. You don't have to agree with the other person, but understanding them goes a long way into improving relationships.

Conclusion

While dealing with difficult people can indeed be difficult, I hope this book was able to help you to know how to effectively deal with difficult people; thus, while it is hard, it is not impossible. If you implement the information contained herein, you will skillfully deal with all types of difficult people.

Thank you and good luck!

CPSIA information can be obtained
at www.ICGtesting.com
Printed in the USA
LVHW081550010821
694264LV00014B/514